A Life of Prayer: Devotions & Pandemic

By

Erwin K Thomas

A Life of Prayer: Devotions & Pandemic

Text copyright © 2021 by Erwin K. Thomas, Ph.D.

United States Copyright Office

Printed in the United States of America by Erwin K. Thomas, Ph.D.

Independent Publisher

First Paperback Edition: February 2021

ISBN – 13: 9780996612593

To my wife Mary, son Matthew, and
daughter-in-law Shannon

Other Works by Erwin K Thomas

Sunlit Streams of Water: Devotions for Religious Naturalists

Dfurstane's Spiritual Beliefs

Heaven Bound: Bread of Life

Guyana's Seawall Girl

Life's Passages: From Guyana to America

Gifts of God: Reflections & Affirmations

Keys of Faith: Fifty-Two Meditations for Living

A Weekly Encounter: Fifty-Two Meditations of Hope

Mass Media in 2025: Industries, Organizations, People, and Nations with Brown H. Carpenter

Handbook on Mass Media In The United States: The Industry and Its Audiences with Brown H. Carpenter

Make Better Videos with Your Camcorder

Contents

Part II - Water People Drink

Part III - Fire People Light

Part IV – Love People Share

Part V – Life People Experience

Part VI – Peace People Explore

Part VII – Hope People Embrace

Introduction

A Life of Prayer is empowering. It fulfills its role with the spirit of love as people walk in God's creation. It focuses on the Supreme Light that enlightens their hearts and minds with the depth of the divine truth. Moreover, prayer motivates believers to have an unconditional love for their neighbors.

Through devotion the earth heals. Disruptions and eruptions from natural phenomena – earthquakes, hurricanes, volcanoes, and wildfires become natural again. Miracles abound, and there's hope. Believers as they do homage to God, Allah, Brahma, and Dao sanctify their environment – homes, communities, and the world. With these blessings they discover God's peace that surpasses all understanding.

Prayer ushers in a renewal of life, and seeds of joy blossom throughout the earth. The sick are healed. The lame walk and believers help the poor with their unique gifts. People live in confidence. They embrace a balanced life with healthy bodies by adhering to a sensible diet and doing physical exercise. Their lives are blessed with an eternal abundance in a quest of purity. Believers develop compassionate hearts that empathize with the down-trodden. Often these precious ones invoke the sacred, meditate on the scriptures, and perform religious rites. These individuals embrace the mysteries of God, renew their minds, and live in peace. Eventually, they become pure souls in their spiritual quest.

A Life of Prayer: Devotions & Pandemic is presented in several parts of this book.

Part I – Air People Breathe

Part II – Water People Drink

Part III – Fire People Light

Part IV – Love People Share

Part V – Life People Experience

Part VI – Peace People Explore

Part VII – Hope People Embrace

These devotions cover a wide variety of topics, and conclude with a prayer.

Erwin K Thomas

PART I - AIR PEOPLE BREATHE

Wear a Mask

Wearing a mask

Is important for saving lives

It's easy to do

And isn't an infringement

On an individual personal freedom

It's amazing what a piece of cloth can do.

Some argue if you have difficulty breathing

You shouldn't be wearing such a mask

But its inconvenience is minimal

It's true a mask will affect how you look

But you can have fun while wearing it

Know that you will be protecting

Others from being infected with the virus

People wear masks of different colors

They are each designed in unique ways

Some are more sophisticated with special filters

But they should cover the mouth and nose

At times it's difficult trying to keep on a mask

While trying to talk to someone

People will be unable to read your lips

But still they can understand what you say

Masks should go with social distancing

"God, help us during this pandemic. Let us realize that by wearing a mask we are protecting others by not spreading the coronavirus. Let us practice social distancing when doing so. These two actions will go a long way in preventing the spread of the virus."

Amen

The Promised Land

Fresh air is refreshing

When the wind blows

It heightens people's spirit

And they come alive

But what can you expect?

Sometimes a strong wind

Will cause them to stumble

This wind of change is around us

What does it mean?

Are people going to be blown away?

Do their beliefs matter anymore?

Or, must they hold the line?

It's a fierce wind blowing across the country

Unprecedented change is in the air

Where do people stand?

Which way are they leaning?

You might ask the question,

"Do I have to choose?"

"Certainly," the answer is "Yes!"

It does matter where you stand

Our nation's future is at stake

"Great Spirit, guide our steps as we traverse any unknown territory. Show us the light to the promised land where people will live in peace."

Amen

Speaking in Tongues

Glossolalia – speaking in tongues

Is alive in some Christian churches

Some believers view these occurrences

As the utterance of God in his people

Some might see it as a mountaintop experience

As the fruits of God centered on a life of the Spirit

Others feel such gifts as many things –

Ecstasy, emotional illumination, morally transforming,

Charismatic, miraculous, or as a religious awakening

But all these gifts are like the air people breathe

It's as though mankind is truly free in an embodied state

If they know God as the true agent

And realize they themselves are powerless to do anything

So some churches teach their members to pray in tongues

This is true of Pentecostals and Charismatic congregations

But there are some denominations divided over this practice

Southern Baptists believe this gift ended

With the death of the Christ's apostles

Jehovah's Witness says this experience isn't of the Holy Spirit

Some hold those who speak in tongues don't believe in the devil

While a few churches advise their members

To refrain from speaking in tongues

Because it will frighten or offend others

"Almighty Protector – author of all gifts, help us to discern what's true and false. Make us realize that believers could be gifted in different ways. And that all don't have to be ministers, apostles, prophets, or teachers, but they could be distinctly blessed."

Amen

Climate Week 2020

Climate Week 2020 has dawned

With companies pledging

To reduce their greenhouse gas emissions

Many of them have eagerly stepped up to the plate

Walmart would become carbon neutral

They plan on planting trees in the environment

This is the way that many of these companies are planning

To meet their targets to improve the quality of life

Other companies that sell food join the bandwagon

These firms will have suppliers cut their food waste

But these goals won't be immediate

They plan to take decades to accomplish them

Excess foods end up in landfills and produce methane

That's known as a supercharged greenhouse gas

Major institutions have endeavored to join this endeavor

In America these are large investment companies

That will let their affiliates know

They should more fully disclose risks

About how they plan to handle their climate emissions

General Electric will no longer build coal-fired power plants

Such power from these plants are steadily declining

As consumers are turning to other means for electricity

BP's growth on oil is decreasing because of less demand

While Morgan Stanley has taken a stance against its investors

Who have relied on fossil-fuel projects as investments

For all these commitments these companies have volunteered

However, it's left to be seen if they will keep their word.

"Great Protector, be with these companies that have plans to cut their carbon emissions. Help them with their goals to make their promises become a reality."

Amen

Sandwiched in Quarantine

Have you become part of a sandwich generation?

Quarantined because of the pandemic?

And just can't breathe?

Where could you turn for help?

You are a family of working professionals

With young kids to raise

And taking care of a father-in-law with dementia

To complicate matters you live in an apartment

The kids have an active pet dog

With both parents, and three kids who share the same space,

And are stranded at home with no place to go

It's confusion for the parents with Zoom meetings

That are taking place throughout the days of the week

There's kids homework to do online that's required

And an elderly grandpa to care for

Grandpa is also suffering from Parkinson's disease

11 million people nationwide are multigenerational caregivers

These caregivers spend some 22 hours a week providing help

A 2019 report by the National Alliance of Caregiving

And Caring across Generations shows one-third of these families

Reporting emotional distress, and a high level of financial strain

But the Family and Medical Leave Act may help

If workers are able to take up to 12 weeks of unpaid family leave

In a 12 month period for qualified family needs

Also Congress passed the Families First Coronavirus Response Act

That requires certain employers to give more paid leave

To persons affected by the coronavirus outbreak

"Omniscient Provider, help all those affected by the coronavirus outbreak to find relief. And heal the nations of the world and Americans affected by this scourge."

Amen

Risks of Retirement

Talking about being able to breathe

And not suffocating in old age

Just look at the risks

Facing those that retire

Whether it's at age 55, 65, or 70

Wenliang Hou, an economist

At the Center for Retirement Research of Boston College

Identified the risks of a typical retiree:

■ How long will a retiree live?

A lot of this projection has to do with

Whether an individual dies at a younger age

Or lives to be quite old by outliving the retirement funds

■ How are the markets doing?

A great deal depends on if the returns

Of the stock market on the investments are strong or weak

■ What is the nature of a retiree's health?

An individual's health can be a tricky business

No one knows if a retiree will enjoy good health

Or if he or she will be dogged with chronic health problems

■ What are the challenges faced by families?

Some families throughout their lives are economically independent.

While a few might suffer the death of a spouse

And others unforeseen circumstances that are problematic

■ Would there be policy risks?

Imagine if there are cuts to Social Security benefits

Or if the family insurance company is bankrupt

"Universal Provider, help retirees that have established safety nets with the funds they need to live in retirement. Protect their investments from the whims of market-fluctuations and bankruptcies."

Amen

Prepare to Die

The pandemic has struck.

It has driven fear in our hearts.

Many thousands have died.

And several millions have been afflicted.

This brings this caregiver to this question:

"Are you prepared to die?"

What's the sensible thing to do?

During this crisis many have died alone in hospitals

Not being able to say "goodbye" to loved ones

With the coronavirus the unexpected happens

So you can at least plan ahead for any eventualities

You never know when your life will be snuffed out.

Why don't you start death planning today?

Make sure your estate planning documents are in order.

You'll need a will and a designated power of attorney.

There are web services such as Lantern that will assist you

To navigate the hoops of your Last Will and Testament

You don't have to wait until you're a senior.

Some individuals in their prime have died unexpectedly.

They have died in accidents, from cancer, and heart disease.

So, don't delay in letting your loved ones know your wishes

"Omnipotent Provider, remove from our hearts the desire to put off death planning issues. Help us so that our loved ones will know our wishes and be provided for in our Last Will and Testament."

Amen

Journalism on Trial

Journalism is on trial

News and information have been hijacked

There's spin on the right and left

One only has to turn on their TV

To Fox News, MSNBC, or CNN

But there are also many imitators

On radio and print media

The Communications Act of 1934 –

Media outlets operated under

In the "public interest, convenience, and necessity"

The law of the land for more than 60 years

Have been overhauled in unprecedented ways

Glimmerings of these changes were on the horizon

In the 1970s and 1980s with a combination

Of technological changes and court decisions

That has given way to the Telecommunications Act of 1996

This sweeping Act allowed fewer, but larger corporations

To operate more media enterprises – relaxing cross ownership rules

What did this mean for local media?

Local media across the communities in America

Were then gobbled up by large corporations

Their news and information departments were impacted

As they consolidated, cut departments, and reporting staff

Filling niches that were ideologically based to increase their profits

These actions affected the major media networks – electronic and print media.

The news values taught at departments of journalism have fallen away.

"Omniscient Provider, help news and information departments to diversify. May the CEOs of these operations look at the content reaching the communities of the nation and not be solely influenced by profits."

Amen

Religious Naturalism

Religious naturalism

Is like a breath of fresh air.

Unlike the monotheistic faiths –

Judaism, Christianity, and Islam

Religious naturalists don't believe

In sin, heaven, or the resurrection

Naturalists focus on scientific proof

About how all aspects of the universe works

Religious naturalists see the world as "sacred"

They extol the millions of galaxies

That adorn the night sky –

The moon, stars, and planets of all sizes

Those we can see, and those that are unseen

They celebrate the cyclical seasons of the year –

Spring, summer, fall, and winter

And all the wonders of our daily lives –

The air we breathe, the water we drink,

And the fire we light to be warm in winter

With religious naturalists "faith" and "hope"

Are based on scientific proof

This religious orientation always acknowledges

The "sacred" as opposed to the "profane"

People are considered in a real way

Interrelated with other species of the world

And there isn't a hierarchical structure the way Westerners think

For religious naturalists don't consider themselves better than other species

And when it comes to an afterlife people, like everything else in nature

Will merge and be one with all the other elements of the universe

"Ultimate Reality, help us to fully understand the cycle of life. Let us be able to see ourselves as part of nature, and realize that when we die we'll be absorbed to become one with the vast universe."

Amen

Fearsome Hurricanes

Since the late 19th century

Hurricanes have killed about 30,000 people

And have caused billions of dollars in destruction

Hurricanes in 2020 were no different

From Hanna in July, Isaias and Laura in August

These were vicious storms which brought massive flooding

Property damage, death, and destruction

These fierce winds are heart-wrenching

In cases homes are blown away

Communications are seriously disrupted

And many fallen trees are strewn throughout the land

Response of local, state and the federal governments

Have been particularly hampered by these massive destructions

Hurricanes Irma and Katrina have caused immense suffering

Throughout the parishes of New Orleans and damages were
   deplorable

There has been such tremendous loss of jobs and livelihoods

Such destruction has literally wiped away the dreams of many locals

Still people continue to pray for relief to counter these devastations

"Omnipotent Creator, our lives are in your hands. Help us to handle the storms of life. When there's destruction comfort us, and be with us so that we can rebuild, and return to normalcy."

Amen

Air Pollution

Solid particles and gases mix

In the air to form pollution

This mixture of hazardous substances

Includes both human-made sources

And is the result of nature

Our vehicles are culprits which emit fumes

Oils and natural gases play their part

By-products of manufacturing generators

Also cause problems in communities

So does coal-fuelled power plants

And the fumes from chemical production

These are all human-made pollution

Nature is also to be blamed

When it releases hazardous substances in the air

These come from the smoke of wildfires

Ash and gases when volcanoes erupt

Gases such as methane

From decomposing organic matter in the soil

These pollutions affect our health.

Lung development is impaired

That leads to emphysema, asthma,

And other chronic ailments like COPD

Cardiovascular disease becomes a problem

Fine particulate matter can impair blood vessel function

And speeds up calcification in arteries

Breast cancer shows up in women

Often living near major roadways

*"Loving God, help us to understand the risks caused by pollutants.
Give us the insight to take the necessary precautions in the way we treat
our environment."*

Amen

Smoking Health Risks

Smoking is bad.
It endangers a person's health
And causes some known problems

In women who become pregnant
Smoking can have an effect on their baby's life
They can have a preterm delivery
A baby can be still-born
Or suffer from low birth weight

Smoking can also affect a man's sperm count.
Women who smoke can have weaker bones.
Smoking affects the health of one's teeth and gums.
Cataracts can show up
And smoking is known to cause diabetes

But people who quit smoking can reap some benefits.
They are able to cut down on cardiovascular disease.
Their risk of having a stroke will be reduced.
Not smoking prevents cancers of the mouth from developing.
The risk of dying from lung cancer is decreased.

"Great Advocate, help those that smoke deal wisely with this problem.
Let them take the necessary steps to ward off disease caused by this habit."

Amen

Let Truth Prevail

The United States is at a crossroads.

Truth is on the line

The election of 2020 has focused on this truth

Still dark forces continue to deny this fact

More than 140-million voters have spoken

The results are clear

There wasn't any massive fraud

But still the Trump administration

Has decided not to recognize Biden as the winner

Democracy is in peril

False insinuations only undermine

The cherished ideals of the U.S. Constitution

It's time for justice to prevail

This is necessary for peace in the land

Why isn't the Trump administration accepting this reality?

People can only speculate

Is it the desire to overturn a legitimate election?

A POLITICO/Morning Consult poll

Shows 70 percent of Republicans support these false claims

This fact doesn't bode well for the nation's democratic traditions

But all good citizens should embrace the truth

And not fan the flames as the hypocrites do

A smooth transition of power will uphold the nation's ideals

"God help our nation as Americans see "untruths" masquerading as "truth." Banish from our midst all falsehoods that seek to undermine the democratic process."

Amen

Misinformation is Dangerous

News organizations that peddle misinformation undermine our democracy

There's no place for such news in America

America has a history of news presentation being objective

But now the society is polarized by agents that focus on divisiveness

Fox News, Breitbart News, Newsmax, and One America News Network (OANN)

Are known to present their audiences with news of disinformation

Why can't news outfits present information that's fair and credible?

Some may argue that it's the ratings that matter most to these peddlers of untruths

But it's the quest of gaining a foothold in the marketplace that's their life's blood

In the American society elite and liberal organs are known for their readership

These include The New York Times and the Washington Post

But the Wall Street Journal is in the top tier and is conservative

Yet these newspapers have standards that measure up to the ethics of good journalism

These are credible sources of news that have endured as journalism's best for years

Still disinformation has been rampant with the Trump administration

It has undermined the news, put science in a defensive posture, and impact climate change

Polls show some 75 percent of Republican voters believe the 2020 election results to be false

Pro-Trump media continue to peddle this truth although the elections were most credible

This division has far-reaching implications for they will undermine America's democracy

"Almighty God, help the people of this nation to separate truth from untruths. Let them hold close to the tenets that the truth will set them free."

Amen

PART II - WATER PEOPLE DRINK

Warming of Oceans

Oceans are our life blood

Living with water is imperative

Water sustains us in many ways

It isn't only the sea creatures that are important

But how these waters are used to traverse between vast continents

Billions of tons of heat-trapping gases are in the atmosphere

These are the work of humans' industrialized age

Our oceans however absorb these gases

The temperature of these waters rise

And marine life such as sea lions, fish, and lobsters are affected

Heat waves cause toxic algae in the seas to grow

The sources of food for marine life die off or migrate

And such heat waves have caused extreme weather patterns

On the West Coast California has experienced drought

Heat has the effect of allowing stagnant air to warm the oceans

Storms are formed by heat waves

In 2018 the Gulf Coast was hit by the tropical storm Gordon

This storm generated by heat impacted cold water

It mixes with warm water to cause unpredictable weather conditions

In 2020 Michael was a tropical cyclone

Which built to hurricane force winds

Killing over 60 people in Florida

"*Universal Spirit, help our scientific efforts in combatting climate change. Guide the work of scientists and citizens alike that they will have a handle in fighting unpredictable weather patterns.*"

Amen

Infected Water

Infected water can kill

It's known to have killed dogs, cattle, and other animals

Dangerous is cyanobacteria that produce neurotoxins

Animals are affected when they drink

And swim in this polluted water

In 2020 some 365 elephants were stricken

In Botswana's Okavango Panhandle

Many of these elephants

In the herd seemed disoriented, and collapsed

Some died suddenly as they walked in circles

But what causes cyanobacteria?

Elevated waste levels

Of phosphate and nitrate are the culprits

They are the reason for this slimy red film

Lack of proper water circulation

And the use of old light bulbs in aquariums

How can a gardener prevent cyanobacteria?

It's best to use recommended dosages of fertilizers

Reduce the run off in the environment

Take care to maintain the household septic tank

Have a buffer of natural vegetation around ponds

And lakes to filter incoming water

"Eternal Essence, help us in making our environment safe for animals.
Give us the knowledge to be able to counter the threat of cyanobacteria
in our streams."

Amen

Rescue of Whales

In 2020 whales were stranded
The largest incident of beaching
On a sandbank in Tasmania
In the rugged Macquarie Harbor
Rescuers were able to save 108
Out of the 470 that were helpless

This task has been difficult
Rescuers had to brave chilly waters
In order to guide the saved ones
Back into the sea
Many of these freed whales
Included adults and calves

The bodies of the less fortunate
Were corralled off and protected
Into enclosed pods with water booms
From being attacked by sharks
These dead ones were later towed
Out to be deposited into the sea

Whales are very friendly creatures

They are highly social

That's why such a large group

Ended up on this sandy embankment

They must have followed a dying matriarch

"Almighty Creator, give us the wisdom to protect whales. As part of the dolphin family, help us understand more about their bonding. Guide us to do all in our power to save them when they are trapped."

Amen

Holy, but Dirty Water

Holy, but dirty water can kill believers

When they submerge themselves

In the Jordan River to be baptized

Or, wash in the Ganges River

As part of a ceremonial rite

Many people might be unaware

That these waters are polluted

They are filled with human waste, and chemicals

From agricultural, and industrial waste

This is the case of the Jordan River

That flows southward through northern Israel

Where John the Baptist baptized Jesus Christ

The same is true for India's Ganges River

Which flows from the Himalayas

With raw sewage

And remains of cremated corpses

Chemical dyes from tanneries

And animal carcasses

Yet Hindus fulfill their religious duties

By submerging themselves in this water

Infectious diseases could be spread

Through contaminated water

Such as typhoid, cholera, paratyphoid fever,

Dysentery, jaundice, and malaria

From chemicals and pesticides

These pollutants are dangerous

To believers' nervous systems

And could even cause cancer

"Eternal One, help believers to be wise in safeguarding their health, for God or Brahma might bless them, but won't prevent illness, or death."

Amen

Journalists Thirst for News

Oh what it means to be informed

To pour over sources seeking understanding

Weighing and considering the facts

Being knowledgeable about what they do

This is the way journalists make their living

Many get their news from wire services

Such as Reuters, AP, and UPI

But the dedicated venture into the fields

Where they hear both sides of a story

Trying to determine the truth

The truth may come by presenting facts

Journalists should endeavor to be objective

But sometimes being subjective has its place

This may well be the best way

By which they present some stories about life

So journalists may wear many hats

These writers may well be historians, literature buffs,

Sociologists, psychologists, or scientists

However many specialize with their stories

They may be ardent sports reporters

Writing columns about one of the many sports

"Great Creator, people are blessed with journalists whose job it is to report the news. Help these writers to present accurate accounts of stories they cover for their communities."

Amen

God's Wisdom & Mercy

God's wisdom and mercy are indescribable

For the Divine is known for infinite grace

Christian believers have an apostolic Spirit

They embrace this eternal gift for spiritual growth

That's seen as an unquenchable fire

A devotee of this Universal Essence says,

"Don't go where the path may lead,

But go instead where there's no path

And be sure to leave a trail"

Contemplating God is great

For people experience goodness, and mercy

Love heals wounded hearts

So when you witness think about God's omnipotence

For this is how to touch unfaithful people

In your pastoral outreach love all mankind

Be industrious and walk in the light

And be devoted believers of the Word

For its God's wisdom

"Almighty God, grant us the peace that passes all understanding. Let our words be soothing to all we encounter during our earthly sojourn."

Amen

Rainwater Harvesting

Rainwater harvesting is a source

For collecting run-off water

From structures for later use

This process can be simple

Such as using a barrel

Or a huge cistern on the landscape

This idea conjures up memories of farms

But such harvesting has become

An alternative to having a water supply

This supply can be for a household or business.

It isn't only used for farms that depend on water.

In many countries such as Germany and Australia

Rain harvesting has become the norm

And it's growing in the United States

This collection of water is known by many names –

Rainwater harvesting, rainwater collection,

And rainwater catchment

But this water collection is a viable alternative

For use in an urban environment

All that a user requires is being able

To capture free water falling on their roof

And directing the flow into a storage tank

This collected water supply will replace

A substantial portion of their water needs

It can supply their whole household

And all that's needed for the landscape

"Merciful Provider, water is essential for living. Help us so that we are able to use this blessing of harvesting to supply our household and landscape needs."

Amen

Rainwater Harvesting Advantages

Rainwater is clean and absolutely free.

With rainwater harvesting users

Have control over the supply

It's especially beneficial to communities

Which have restrictions on their water

Rainwater harvesting is socially acceptable

And is environmentally friendly to the landscape

The rainwater is best for plants and gardens

Because this runoff isn't chlorinated

Use of rainwater reduces storm water runoff

From homes and businesses in the community

It solves drainage problems many cities have

While it provides an abundance of free water

Rainwater harvesting uses simple technology

Which isn't expensive or cumbersome

It can be used as a main source of water

For wells and municipal water systems

This system can be easily retrofitted

To an existing structure for its benefits

This allows for expansion, reconfiguration

And relocation of this source of water supply

It provides for a useful backup of water

"Omniscient Provider, thank you for the benefits that water harvesting provides. Help us to use such water wisely in our homes and gardens."

Amen

Collected Rainwater

Rainwater is a vital source.

It can be used in many ways.

It's different from tap water

That's chlorinated

But it can be used like tap water

No longer would you have to use

Tap water to flush toilets and water lawns

Such use is irresponsible

In light of population growth and water shortages

Rainwater collection is to green your home

And lessen your indoor and outdoor use

Your new environmental footprint will be appreciated

So it's good to install a water harvesting system

With a water harvesting system

You can hand-water your lawn and garden

After you connect this device to the irrigation/sprinkler system

Use rainwater instead of tap water to wash your car

Refill your swimming pool from your water collection

Wash off your driveway and sidewalk with such water

Use this rainwater for all personal uses when filtered and disinfected

"Great Designer, you have shown us new ways of collecting rainwater for our daily use. Help us to use this water wisely and economically to satisfy our daily needs."

Amen

Drought in Communities

What a dilemma people face

When the land on which they live

Dries up and there isn't anywhere to turn

This has happened in parts of the United States.

Africa, Asia, Middle East, and Latin America

Having enough water is the problem

Rivers, lakes, and streams run dry

And farmers have no place to turn

To water their crops that have to be irrigated

So their trees, plants, and vines don't die

Farmers who are raising animals suffer

Their cows, pigs, horses, and chickens

Cry out for help, but there isn't any water

The ground is baked dry by relentless sunshine

And water has ceased flowing to their plots

This novel form of drought that has emerged

Reaches to the width and depth of the earth

It's the result of shifting oceans and atmospheric patterns

This situation has developed because of expanding human water needs

This crisis is due to the ecological impact of humans' demand on water

"Eternal Provider, help people live in communities where their need for water will be met. And when there's drought, make other sources of water become accessible."

Amen

PART III - FIRE PEOPLE
LIGHT

The Elite Media

John C. Merrill wrote The Elite Press

Noam Chomsky said, "It's the agenda-setting media"

That sets "the framework in which everyone else operates"

Media such as the New York Times, Washington Post,

And the Wall Street Journal are elite newspapers

CBS, NBC, and ABC are TV networks

Which also come to mind

So are PBS, CNN, and Fox News

But all these news sources are controlled by corporations

They are in the business of selling audiences

But there's a difference with these news organizations

Some are considered right-wing

While others are said to lean to the left

Chomsky is thought of as being on the left

Bill O' Reilly of Fox News is on the right side of the spectrum

The New York Times and CBS appeal to a privileged group –

Managers, corporate executives, and university professors

While Fox News influences right-wing

Opinion leaders, evangelicals, and conservatives

Time and Newsweek stand out as magazines of prominence.

But all the elite sources are battling the rise of misinformation

That has been more prevalent throughout the Trump administration

Politico has found 70 percent of Republicans believe

The 2020 elections results between Trump and Biden to be false

But the elite press and social media are pushing to clear the air of such distortions

"God, grant us the insight to determine what's true in the market place of ideas. Help American media officials to counter all falsehood with their political stories, by presenting the facts to their audience."

Amen

Symbolism of Fire

Fire is an emblem of divinity, political, and social unity

For millions of years with fire our ancestors kept warm

It protected them from being attacked by wild animals

Served as a meeting place for tribal communities

Where religious rites such as chanting and telling stories were performed

Most importantly after a hunt hunters cooked their meals

Ancient traditions glorify fire

In the Hindu tradition the goddess Shiva –

Destroyer, transformer, maintainer, and preserver is depicted as dancing in a circle of fire

The Book of Exodus describes Moses's encounter with a burning bush

Classical Greek mythology shows how Promethius –

The champion of mankind stole fire from the gods to give to humans

Acts of the Apostles reminded Christian believers

How the Holy Spirit appeared to the disciples as flames of fire

In ancient Persia and Rome fire played a prominent role

The Zoroastrian religion made use of fire, and clean water to represent ritual purity

While priests tended the eternal fires on fire-altars

In the Roman religion Vestal was the Roman goddess of the hearth

Who was the protectorate

And were served by chaste Vestal Virgins

Today Paris burns a flame of national significance

It's known as The Eternal Flame at the Arc de Triomphe

John F. Kennedy's Eternal Flame symbolizes eternal life

While the flame at the War Memorial

Shows Americans' profound gratitude towards the remembrance

Of our dead service men and women

"Almighty Creator, help us to understand more fully the use of fire. Let us be always blessed by the good things it signifies."

Amen

Banned Books

Writers are brilliant thinkers

They put their souls into their works

Yet some of these World Voices are banned

And PEN America has championed their cause

Also the American Library Association

2020 witnessed book bans

In Alaska, Tennessee, and Missouri

It therefore becomes essential to advocate

To safeguard the right to read

Institutions – libraries and schools shouldn't

Be in the business of censoring books

Librarians, booksellers, publishers,

Journalists, teachers, and readers

Should be promoting the nation's authors

Books by John Bolton and Mary Trump

The American government has attempted to block

Banned Book Week focused on such restrictions

It advocates for the access to all books

And abhors censorship of any kind

It calls attention to the harm censorship does

Banned Books Week was launched in the 1980s

During a time of challenges and protests

With the 1982 Supreme Court case

Of Island Trees School District v. Pico

That ruled school officials can't ban books

In libraries because of their content

"Universal Advocate, guide the leaders of this land to uphold people's right to reading materials of all kind. Give advocates the freedom to speak out against all forms of censorship in order that the readers will have recourse to the whole body of creative works."

Amen

Wildfires in the West

In the summer months of 2020

Hot weather has renewed

Dangers of wildfires in the West

Extreme heat is causing

Many trees to burn

And the West Coast is experiencing

Intense cases of fires

Sweeping over millions of acres

Some 170,000 firefighters in California

Are battling 25 of these blazes

But there isn't much they can do

For these fires are just sweeping across the landscape

Of Washington, Oregon, and California

Where dozens have been killed

Scientific evidence shows

Increasing air temperatures and drying soils,

With dead vegetation, and climate change

Increase the frequency for extreme fire risks

Homes built near forested areas

Have also been a very big problem

For wildfires engulf all these buildings

As they are swept along by strong winds

"Ultimate Provider, be with the firefighters in having the tools and know-how to fight such wildfires. Help people so that they will play their part by not building more homes near forested areas."

Amen

Comparative Religions

Comparative religions were shaped

By a euro-centered culture

This formed the basis

Of what students know about world religions

Much of this trajectory was lit by missionaries

They came from Europe and traversed the globe

Many were religious as they encountered colonists

Their basic strands became the bedrock

Of how they interpreted the various religious faiths –

Such as Judaism, Christianity, Islam,

Hinduism, Daoism, Shintoism, and secular humanism

These interpreters ushered in their thoughts about religion

They revived an emphasis in Greek and Latin

That led to the shape of comparative Christianity

Becoming prominent in the Protestant Reformation

Some European theologians became famous –

Martin Luther, John Calvin, and Desiderius Erasmus

But the world of religion was born with the Peace of Westphalia

And by the 17th century there existed a noteworthy guide

That included all the known religions of the world

From the 18th to 21st century there was a broadening of its scope

With peoples of India, China, Russia, Artic and Oceania

In the West Sanskrit studies became popular

And Semitic languages and religions were studied

The Age of Enlightenment dawned

With figures such as Charles Darwin, Sir Isaac Newtown,

And contemporary thinkers such as Richard Dawkins,

Christopher Hitchens and Karen Armstrong

"Great Designer, you have lit a fierce fire in the heart of comparative religions. Grant that this process continues to grow with an enduring flame."

Amen

Light of Life

In revelation deities and saints show goodness, clarity, and insight

And light is also a symbol of purity and openness

The light of Buddhists and Bodihisattvas come from within

It's often depicted as a rainbow or flames above their heads

Showing that they have achieved Enlightenment

In Hinduism light symbolizes Brahman – the eye, self, gods, and divinity

Believers embrace this light as the power of the sun, a star, or planet

Often it's seen as an illumination of the mind, brilliance, happiness, and prosperity

Devout Hindus are inspired by its wisdom, knowledge, intuition, and energy

In Christianity light is a motif that resides within

The humble minds of the faithful Christians are considered enlightened

This light is considered supernatural, and part of their religious life from creation

Believers hold to the tenets that with light the darkness of bad deeds would disappear

Christians are taught to view themselves as the light of the world

By so doing the Angels of Light work on their behalf

Sikhs and Quakers also have a concept of inner light

But all believers are blessed with the light of the stars that twinkle on moonlit nights

They see light in all its dimensions shining brightly revealing the truth of love

With light as instruments of peace believers are blessed with the light of courage

For Christians the Prince of Peace is a savior, teacher, guardian, provider, and flame of hope

"Natural Omnipotence, with light let all religious faiths heal the brokenhearted of the world, by pursuing love, peace, and truth."

Amen

Compulsive Hoarding

Compulsive hoarding is a serious health problem

In its worst form it can cause fires

Rat and cockroach infestations

And other alarming health and safety hazards

Most hoarders may collect a variety of worthless items –

Old catalogues, magazines, and newspapers,

Materials for making crafts, used clothing,

Tables, chairs, or sofas, pots, pans and silverware

That may be trash, cluttered, and beyond repair

Some hoarders are unable to return borrowed objects

And will argue with family members about their clutter

They may be residents of homes with unsanitary bathrooms

So they keep their household shades drawn

To prevent neighbors from seeing inside of their apartment

Hoarding is considered an obsessive-compulsive disorder

Many of these individuals are depressed and anxious

Because of the clutter there are always risks of falling

Their bathtub and sinks are filled with items

That cannot be useful for washing or bathing

Such habits are the result of compulsive acquisition behavior

"Almighty Creator, help hoarders so that their distress and impairment don't become a serious problem that causes an economic burden, and has effects on their family and friends. Bring healing professionals in the lives of these individuals so their lives could be turned around."

Amen

Tropical Wetlands Inferno

Tropical wetlands' fires are staggering in South America

This is happening in the Pantanal that stretches

Over parts of Brazil, Paraguay, and Bolivia

The Pantanal attracts tourists from around the world.

It's the home for breathtaking wildlife

Such as jaguars, tapirs, otters, and macaws

During the rainy season these lands

Fill with water from the torrents of rainstorms

But this year climate change has brought a drought

Fires and food production have wiped away 25 percent of the forest

These fires are raging out of control enveloping trees and animals in
their paths

In the past the flames were controlled by countless swamps, lagoons,
and tributaries

These natural water barriers have all dried up

The forest has become a tinderbox as fires sweep through the land

These fires are the worst in the memory of the Guató people,

An indigenous tribe whose ancestors lived in the region for thousands
of years

These flames have even burned the properties and holdings

Of these peoples who depend on this natural habitat for their
livelihood

*"Great Spirit, help us in our quest to safeguard the Pantanal forest. Guide
all those who work in bringing the indigenous peoples relief and may
these people benefit by their efforts. Also, enable conservationists to do
what they can to safe this vital resource for mankind."*

Amen

Light of Pharaohs

Pharaohs shone their light for all to see

From their civilizations of the Nile Valley

Their history presents a fascination for Egypt

A history and organization of the State

Society and daily life, mythology and religion

Art and culture that shaped the Egyptian way of life

Egyptian Pharaohs enjoyed a dual nature of being divine and human

Their society was modelled on the basis of a caste system

Pyramids embodied the architectural grandeur

Of Egyptian culture, life on planet earth, and the afterlife

Egyptians explored science, and were artistically quite gifted

Many civilizations are indebted to Egypt for its agricultural benefits

For its innovations in the field of medicine, and scientific discoveries

Egypt is known for its murals, classical literature, and philosophy.

All these achievements came from communities on the banks of the
River Nile

On fertile banks were discovered the deposits of the cradle of Egypt's
civilization

That stretched from the 1st to the 8th Dynasty when the first
pyramids were built

From the 9th to the 12th Dynasty that witnessed conflicts between Upper and Lower Egypt

To the 13th Dynasty to decadence after invasions before the Roman conquest

"Omnipotent One, who has witnessed the rise and fall of great civilizations, help us to be cognizant of the Pharaohs' contribution to the world. And let their achievements be as milestones through which nations could appreciate and enhance their living conditions."

Amen

God is Nature

The 17th century Jewish philosopher
Of Dutch origin, Baruch Spinoza, viewed religion
In Theological-political Treatise as superstitious
He considered Nature and God ubiquitous

Nature encompasses all things Spinoza considered Providence
Every aspect of its essence is reflected in good and bad experiences
Miracles described in the monotheistic faiths of Judaism, Christianity
And Islam could be explained through the varieties of ever-changing
  nature
These are natural occurrences that surprise people when such
  phenomena occur

The first rainbow that humans saw must have struck them as a miracle
But science later showed this resulted from scientific evidence
Prophecy could be viewed as another of these phenomena
In ancient times people were uneducated and had vivid imaginations
Many of their delusions were motivated by vivid dreams and visions

In modern society these ancients would be seen as having psychotic
  episodes
But these visionaries appeared to the Israelites as being filled with
  images of a Creator

Therefore God is perceived as being human and personalized

Nature is all things good and bad that exist in the vast Universe

It's more realistic to think about the Divine as Nature by an objective analysis

God in Nature is material and immaterial

God doesn't have human characteristics that are alluded to in sacred texts

This spiritual essence is universal and governs all things

Putting a human face on God of Nature is an error that equates God with humankind

"Divine Creator, who isn't conservative or liberal, help people so that they will promote what's best for the citizenry. Let them see the 20th century treatise and ethics of Spinoza as a visionary work in religion for democracies where free speech is a hallmark."

Amen

Forest Fires' Advantages

Some wildfires are good for forests.

Despite the damages caused

Good things can result

For forests containing dead trees

And decaying plant matter

Fires turn these limbs into ashes

So these nutrients return to the soil

As a result of these wildfires

The forest's floor receives sunlight

This allows the seedlings to sprout

Fires are known to kill diseases

And insects that prey on trees

They provide nutrients that enrich the soil

Wildfires burning in areas

That don't impact humans

Are regenerative to the forest

They revitalize the watershed

Renew the soil, and reset the clock

For an abundant ecosystem

Even the natural wildlife benefits

New trees grow back on their own after wildfires

Forests recover from the fires through germination

Of seeds stored on the floor of the forests

And branches sprout from trees that have been killed

Some of these plants need the heat to germinate

"Universal Provider, let people realize that not all forest fires are bad. Let them see that when wildfires don't impact human developments they provide many good benefits to the forests."

Amen

Forest Fires' Disadvantages

When people think about wildfires

They recall the damage and devastation

Caused to wildlife and vegetation

A positive condition takes a long time to return

It was estimated that the Brazilian Atlantic forest

Would take some 65 years to regrow

For the landscape to return to its original shape

Will take up to some 4000 years

But there are other immediate disadvantages

These wildfires can destroy homes, lives,

And millions of acres of forest

The aftermath of these fires can be worse.

Fires burn trees and plants that prevent erosion

The ill-effects of forest fires could be caused by humans

Natural fires are generally started by lightning

Small amount of fires are caused by spontaneous combustion

Of dried fuel such as sawdust and decaying leaves

Human-caused fires could be due to a variety of reasons

Forest fires can start in any part of the world

But they are most common in forested areas

Many places are susceptible to these fires including

The United States, vegetated areas in Australia,

As well as the Western Cape of South Africa

"Universal Spirit, help people's understanding of the ill-effects of forest fires. Let us do what's right to minimize the harm that the wildfires may cause."

Amen

PART IV - LOVE PEOPLE SHARE

Vote Your Conscience

Vote as if your life depends on it

Our country is going through cataclysmic changes

There's divisiveness, racial tension, and grand-standing

The United States Supreme Court has lost a key judge

In justice Ruth Bader Ginsburg

It isn't only for us to elect senators and congress persons

Americans have to choose governors, mayors, and other state officials

So be sure to send a message to protect our democracy

Let there always be checks and balances

For our country's future is at stake

Understanding why citizens will want to vote is clear

Every four years they get a chance to select officials

Some may not feel that their vote counts much

They argue that they are only one in millions

But shouldn't citizens all try to pull together?

It's true others might believe in the serenity prayer

That people should do what they can

They should know the difference when they can't

That's when situations are beyond their influence

Nevertheless people should do whatever is in their power

To make good governance available to future generations

In this endeavor they should commit themselves

"Universal Creator, cleanse our hearts and help us as voters. Guide us so that we do what's right by voting our conscience. Remove fear and intimidation from our desire to uphold the tenets of democracy."

Amen

The Good Cyclist

Cyclists share the road and trails with others

They should ride in the direction of the traffic

And be mindful that they're slower than motorized vehicles

It isn't unusual for riders to use the sidewalks

But it's for them to make way for pedestrians

So it's important to ride slowly

It's always wise to be courteous on a trail

Be respectful to people with walkers and animals

If you have to pass them do so carefully

You may ring your bell to alert pedestrians of your presence

It make no sense to be huffing and puffing as you ride

With riding it ought to be remembered that safety is a prime
concern

Undoubtedly the coronavirus pandemic has brought more concerns

Cyclists have to be prepared for eventualities by wearing masks

You never know when you'll encounter a fellow traveler

It's also wise to be always prepared to disinfect your bike

Bikeshare regularly does this with cycles in their company

And it should be remembered that riders should have a helmet

As a cyclist you're required to be healthy

Do your research if you have to venture into unknown territory

And with Covid-19 it's best to practice social distancing

So on your trips you'll be better able to enjoy the fresh air and scenery

"Ultimate Reality, be with us as we traverse the landscape on our bicycles. Help us to do so safely with regard to the motorized traffic, and with pedestrians on the sidewalks and trails."

Amen

A Therapy Pet

A therapy pet can be one of a number of animals –

Dogs, cats, llamas, miniature pigs, mini-horses, or birds

But many people choose dogs

Dogs could be emotional support dogs

Therapy, and certified service dogs

But why are these dogs necessary?

Many people attest to the benefits of having such pets

Because they lift their mood, relieve stress

And help them recover from health problems

In hospitals and mental institutions

Classrooms are also a good place for such dogs

Students benefit during physical exercise

Interactions with these dogs lower blood pressure

And having them around are stimulating

For they assist students and patients with pain management.

But there's a difference between a "therapy dog" and "service dog."

A therapy dogs helps their clients physically and emotionally,

While a service dog perform tasks

Those individuals are unable to do themselves

"God, help us to use the pets of your creation in beneficial ways. Teach us the best ways to use such animals to serve mankind. And help us to treat these pets with love and kindness for the work they do."

Amen

Lives of the Disabled

Disabilities impact some of our citizens.

They suffer emotionally, physiologically, and psychologically.

But these individuals aren't spiritually disabled.

Help the disabled concentrate on things

That their disabilities don't prevent them from doing

They shouldn't regret the things they can't do

In ancient Jewish society lepers were considered unclean

They were forced to live in segregated communities

Many Jewish citizens viewed these disabled persons as unclean

But there were those brave caregivers that socialized with them

And their acts annoyed many in the Jewish communities

Some of the religious leaders were angered

Christian theologians teach about the redemptive nature of suffering

Disabled believers should walk in the light and offer up their suffering to God

Yet in contemporary times persons with disabilities are portrayed negatively

They are often shown as criminals, sexual abusers, thieves, and portrayed as violent

On the media viewers have seen such depictions in films and TV

It's therefore wise to correct these negative depictions about the disabled

Instead why don't media show the work of caregivers, mental health workers?

And drug and alcohol specialists working to help these afflicted individuals

Viewers should stop seeing the disabled as victims

"Omnipotent Caretaker, show us useful ways of dealing with those that are disabled. Help us in unique ways to treat their problems. And guide us in promoting their gifts that are beneficial to our nation."

Amen

Food Waste

By 2030 some of the largest food suppliers

Have pledged to cut their food waste in half

Companies such as Rice Krispies cereal, Hellmann's mayonnaise

And Spam have joined the 10x20x30 initiative

An effort to slash the amount of food discarded yearly

The process will involve companies making annual reports

They will center on the sharing of information about food waste

As a Dannon executive stated that this would explore all options

The goal is to turn wasted foods into animal food or compost

Food waste has always been a sore point in the industry

And Walmart, Kroger, and Giant Foods have embraced similar pledges

They have enlisted their suppliers to commit to their plans

These food companies hope to accomplish such objectives set

By the United Nations General Assembly by 2015, to halve food waste

According to the United Nations Food and Agriculture Organization

The supply chain throws away about 30 percent of the world's food

This waste is a great contributor to the world's climate change problem

This produce amounts to about 10 percent of the global greenhouse
   gas emissions

So the food manufacturing industry is a player in climate change

It has been reported about 80 percent of waste food comes from

Homes, manufacturers, grocery stores, and restaurants

These sources can do more by limiting such productions

By having consumers not toss out the excess in their daily lives

There should be a system that will enable them not to act badly

*"Divine Provider, help food producers to curb their waste. And let
consumers realize that they have a responsibility to make more sensible
decisions about the way they use their food."*

Amen

Mexican Migrants' Love

Mexican migrants take the responsibility

Of loved ones back in Mexico seriously

That's why they send remittances

To keep their families fed

And help to provide for their medical needs

Billions of dollars are received by the Bank of Mexico

From immigrants working as fruit and vegetable field hands

These migrants earn as much as $80 U.S. dollars per day

It was thought that the pandemic would have eclipsed their efforts

But still these workers have shown resilience to feed their families

48 percent of Mexicans aren't earning enough in their own country

What they are paid isn't able to buy a basic basket of food

In Mexico there aren't jobless benefits or Medicare

And workers and businesses have received little relief during the
  pandemic

But low-income Mexican field workers in the United States

Play a very important role in helping their families in desperate need

Despite the back-breaking work in the fields of America

These field hands have stepped up to the plate

By undertaking such altruistic roles in helping those back home

"Loving God, continue to help the Mexican field hands to be good providers for their families in Mexico. Be with them as they labor and keep them safe from harm."

Amen

Paralympics Games 2020

Tokyo 2020 Paralympics Games

Are set for August 24 to September 5, 2021

This postponement resulted

From the coronavirus pandemic

That's sweeping through nations

Paralympic athletes compete in different sports.

These range from archery, athletics, and badminton

To team sports like football, basketball, and rugby

Paralympic Football is an adaptation of association football

Wheelchair Rugby is a contact sport for players with disabilities

These disability athletes compete in groups –

Amputee, cerebral palsy, visual impairment,

Spinal cord injuries, intellectual disability

And those disabilities that don't fit the previous categories

It's similar in grouping athletes by age, gender or weight

Paralympic athletes train with a coach

They are geared to meet the standards of their group

And are taught about their competition requirements

These basic procedures make them eligible to compete

"Omniscient One, you have created each person with a unique potential. Help the disabled during summer and winter to compete and bond with other competitors in the spirit of these sports."

Amen

World Food Program

In 2020 the World Food Program

A Rome-based United Nations agency

Won the Nobel Peace Prize

This UN agency combats hunger around the world

It's active in nations that are torn by conflicts

This has especially been the case since the pandemic

That has brought millions of people to the brink of starvation

The United States has pulled out of several UN bodies

These include the Human Rights Council

And UNESCO, the cultural agency

The World Health Organization has come under attack

Over the way it was handling the coronavirus pandemic

The Trump administration will leave the UN next July

The U.S. has been UN's biggest donor

But the World Food Program and its partners

Put their lives in danger when they go to feed millions

In Yemen, Congo, Nigeria, and South Sudan

Their unprecedented efforts are supported

By nearly 130 countries and are key

To the efforts of bringing aid such as drugs and vaccines

To combat a variety of diseases ravishing poorer nations

"Universal Spirit, continue to bless the efforts of the countries engaged in bringing humanitarian aid to many poor nations and people around the globe. Help the UN World Food Program in their attempts to relieve suffering of an estimated 690 million people struggling with hunger in the world today."

Amen

Home Sweet Home

Americans shouldn't lose track

Of the importance of the home

In their daily lives

A nation's strength begins in the home

Parents should train their children the best way

These values pass down from generation to generation

It's this training that determines the caliber of the nation

If fathers and mothers are lax in these responsibilities

Their children will grow up to dishonor their parents

On the other hand, if they are faithful in raising their children

They will be taught right and be shining lights to the nation

It's for ethnic groups – Black, White, Yellow, and Red

To instill the right moral values in the young

If they fail at this task, they will fail in their duties as citizens

So everyday let your children make you proud

And let your actions ring out concerning how blessed

We are to be living in one of the greatest nations of the earth

Parents will be following in the traditions of our founding fathers

Who conceived this nation in liberty to the proposition

That all men and women are created equal

It's for parents to do their duty to instill these tenets in the young

The quality of the nation rests on the teachings of parents.

"Ultimate Reality, help our families to promote the traditions of equality of all peoples. Especially be with parents in this undertaking, that their children will be blessed, and become shining lights in the nation."

Amen

Indigenous Peoples' Day

September 12th is Indigenous Peoples' Day
In some states this day replaces Columbus Day
So too with many U.S. cities and school districts

States like South Dakota, New Mexico, Vermont
And Maine have officially embraced this day
Other states like Arizona, Virginia, and Oregon
Have recognized this special day
But would continue to celebrate Columbus Day
As a federal holiday

Cities such as Salem, MA, Rockville, MD, Montclair, NJ
Charlottesville, Alexandria, and Richmond, VA
Have made the switch to celebrate indigenous peoples
Bills have been passed in other cities to embrace this trend

Indigenous peoples were the first stewards of America
And they have suffered historical injustices
These peoples have faced persecution
And removal from their homelands by government's actions

It's hoped that other states will follow suit

To rectify past governmental decisions that have impacted American Indians

This will lead the way for a full recognition for partnerships

Between the indigenous peoples, and mutual trust between all citizens

"Great Spirit, help states, cities, and school districts bring to fruition a day honoring the indigenous peoples of the United States. Let us continue to recognize all their contributions as first stewards of these lands."

Amen

Saving Halloween

It has been a trying time with this pandemic

Halloween will come under attack

The way people trick or treat will change

You can expect "contactless" trick or treating

And virtual story telling of ghost stories

Halloween presents its participants with hope

They become embedded in escapism

A feeling believers' need especially during this crisis

But people can still expect storefronts to peddle their wares

The Spirit of Halloween will be on hand with many items

Expect to see costumes and spooky fall décor

In a variety of pop-up locations in the United States

It has opened more than 14-hundred storefronts

Halloween businesses have come to occupy shuttered storefronts

Of companies that have since gone out of business due to the pandemic

So there will be the grim reaper greeting guests in these stores

And sanitizer dispensers with skeletal hands throughout buildings

Although a downturn in sales is to be expected

Still you'll see vampires, cheerleaders, wizards, and ghostly characters

And selected ones in costumes on display will be wearing masks

There will be Tiger King characters and scary marshmallow musicians

"Infinite Designer, help those that are trick or treating explore devilish treats in their neighborhoods. Let this event fill them with hope as they escape the realities of life during this pandemic."

Amen

The Serenity Prayer

Reinhold Niebuhr was author of this prayer.

Since its inception in 1943

The prayer itself has had an interesting history

It was hijacked in Germany

The country where Niebuhr's parents were born

Before settling in the United States

Niebuhr's life was as a preacher, writer, professor,

And ambassador to European countries

Especially Germany and England

He interacted with the World Council of Churches

And shared his thoughts on ecumenical ventures

Of various denominations – Episcopalian, Methodist,

Congregationalist, Reformed, and Evangelical Lutherans

For 40 years Niebuhr was a pastor and professor

At the Union Theological Seminary in New York

He ruffled feathers with his opposition to American neutrality

During World War II, beliefs in racial equality,

And his outreach to the poor in the ghettos

Niebuhr was a guest on panels, was welcomed internationally

On the lecture circuit, known for his correspondence

With Church leaders and lived to see Europe liberated

The serenity prayer captured life's vicissitudes

By how Niebuhr responded to the challenges of his era

"Loving God, you have blessed mankind with the kind spirit of Reinhold Niebuhr. Grant that his legacy will live on as we utter the serenity prayer known worldwide through the Alcoholic Anonymous (AA) meetings, and its many renditions on postcards, placemats, and souvenirs."

Amen

Dressed to Kill

Dressed to kill by wearing glamorous clothes

To create a striking appearance

Is alive and well during this pandemic

When many people are with masks

These new attractions are of different colors

Sizes, shapes, and some have sayings

Are these masks telling us to kill?

Or, are they lessons for not being killed?

These distinct pieces of cloth add to our outfits

People who are wearing them stand out

Some in the younger generation dress attractively

For they may wish to attract a lover

While others care about being in fashion

And wear what it takes to fit in

But there are people who manipulate their bodies

To have desired looks they consider appealing

Some women wear brassieres, corsets, fashionable belts

Or high-heeled shoes to give them that special look

Some individuals would even pierce their ears

To fit in with their peers to have a different appeal

But wearing masks reveal a caring disposition

To all those who are health conscious

And would like to be safe during these troubling times

Masks, social distancing, and washing of hands

Is part of the requirements to be safe during this pandemic

These are rituals people have to do so as to not get infected.

"Universal Provider, let us realize that during this pandemic people should not only dress to be admired, but they should do so by wearing a mask in public places. This is the new way to dress to kill and not risk being killed by the coronavirus. Help us to protect ourselves as best as we can."

Amen

Healing with Love

Do you have constant headaches, low energy, and aching limbs?

Are you nervous with colds and sweaty palms?

Do you have clenched jaws and grind your teeth?

Do you suffer from palpitations and anxiety attacks?

Are you prone to violent outbursts?

Do you have a mental problem, an eating disorder, or are you obese?

Then you could be worn out with the demands of the world

You might have a lack of appetite, addicted to alcohol, or nicotine

Maybe you're pacing the floor, fidgeting, and unable to settle down

With such behavior you're unable to focus on your work

You could even be suffering from some other chronic ailment

But you just can't sleep at night, and have no sexual interest

Your condition might be due to the rat race in the work place

From childhood you were taught to be competitive

"Be your best! The sky is the limit!" You were told

You never knew it, but you were coerced to join the band of competitors

Now you are running on overdrive and hooked on a computer

You just can't find the time to relax and enjoy life

But correct this negative course by embracing positive changes

Be sure to check with your doctor about these impending problems

This will take is a change in your lifestyle before it's too late

Make time to eat right, get a good night's sleep, relax, and exercise
to alleviate the stress

"God, help us with our health problems. Give us the insight to deal with these afflictions so that we would be able to be healthy again. And grant us your love and peace of mind to enjoy our work."

Amen

PART V - LIFE PEOPLE EXPERIENCE

Encroachment of Nature

People have invaded the wilderness

Homes are built besides forests

Trees tower overhead in the distant

And there's constant logging

Mankind has definitely encroached on nature

Wildlife is crying out for help

Creatures of all kinds are losing their habitats

People are now affected

By species carrying viruses

So they are infected with diseases

They never experienced before

CO_2 is heating up the planet

Bringing in its wake unprecedented storms

For months there have been violent winds, rain, and flooding

That has been impacting many Northern and Southern states

Wildfires are raging in the West

Homes and businesses are going up in flames

Thousands are forced to flee

And Washington, Oregon, and California

Are in the throes of such a crisis

People have to be able to live in harmony with nature

"Supreme Spirit, help us learn the best way to be with nature. Enable us to live in harmony with its abundant gifts that surround us."

Amen

Worn-out Workers

Worn-out workers are the ones who do the heavy lifting

They labor in the fields, clean offices, pick up our garbage

And build the highways and byways of life

These workers are on the job from morning 'til night

Their work is hard, redundant, and demanding

Yet their pay and benefits are poor

What is the future of these vulnerable workers?

After toiling many years could there be some relief?

But nothing is ever done to improve the lot of this working class

After struggling on their jobs their bodies wear out

Many of these individuals will fail to reach retirement age

These workers are often dogged with chronic ailments

Some have stiffened knees, sciatica, and back problems

Their minds are willing, but their bodies are weak

What will become of these workers who have done so much for us?

Many just fade away and end up without homes

And the means of taking care of themselves

What can be done in the interest of these poor souls?

They aren't of an age to receive social security and Medicare

There should be social measures to care for this vulnerable population

It's only right to have laws and a safety net to take care of them

"God, help all vulnerable workers that labor in our nation. Guide our legislators and social networks to come to their aid. Let it be known that all lives are important for our society's welfare."

Amen

Save the Pangolin

The pangolin is an endangered specie

Eight of these species

Are protected under international law

Still they are hunted for medicinal properties

This creature is prized in Asia

Although there isn't any evidence

That this scaly mammalian has properties

Beneficial to human health

But what can conservationists do?

They should help save this bizarre little creature

So it doesn't disappear from their environment

For man-made threats are causing mass extinctions

Efforts are made at Save Vietnam's Wildlife

A conservation reservation program

Inside the Cuc Phuong National Park

To save the world's most trafficked mammal

The Vietnamese government has decided

To crack down on this illegal wildlife trade

Researchers have also found in Thailand

That 36 percent of all reptile species

Are often traded on the Internet

About 90 percent are caught in the wild

"Divine Creator, help conservationists to implement programs to safeguard the world's biodiversity. Guide them in their efforts to save creatures like the pangolin."

Amen

African American Cemeteries

Black cemeteries exist nationally

But some are in a state of disarray

Many are located in the South

Names such as the Evergreen and the East End Cemetery

In Richmond, VA, Magnolia in rural eastern Arkansas

And South-View Cemetery in Atlanta, GA

Where Representative John Lewis was buried

These cemeteries were established

During the Civil War

In hazardous, hilly, and wooded terrain

And for decades Black people

Have been migrating from these sites

Moving North and West to escape racial prejudice

But volunteers have manned these burial plots

They did so in segregated times

And expressed pride in these undertakings

South-View Cemetery was chartered in 1886

And have Black businessmen as current board members

Success in endeavoring to maintain these cemeteries

Have a great deal to do with the passion

Such burial plots evoke for the volunteers

Still there are problems with maintenance

Because of lack of funds, enough volunteers,

And having access to older cemetery records

"Great Emancipator, shine your light on the Black souls that are resting in these cemeteries. Let not their lives be forgotten, but their gravesites remain a memorial for future generations."

Amen

Diverse Gifts

God gave us the gift of life

It's for us to give ourselves

The gift of living well

This blessing might not be perfect

But some of the best gifts are free

Some people might have the gift of health

Others might be born with a superb intelligence

But there are those with material abundance

They have become rich beyond comparison

Even if they did suffer from a setback

It's known that those who have a disability

Attributed their accomplishments

To a unique handicap that has dogged them

This disability helped these individuals

To focus on the special talents of their life

Ironically through these unique afflictions

They were able to excel and find happiness

The gift of happiness brings joy

The recipients make people laugh

Just bringing levity to friends is contagious

This is different from having free choice

A blessing that might well be built on love

That drives away fear from our hearts

"Divine Intercessor, teach us ways to use our gifts for the benefit of mankind. Let us realize that even mistakes that people make could well be special blessings."

Amen

Labor Day

Oh what a life!

Having labored all night

What else can I do?

It's best to relax today

And honor all those with jobs

Think of all the days I've worked

To feed my family

Put bread on our table

Helping us live well

If it weren't for my job

We shall surely be on the streets

But today I give "Thanks"

For all the blessings my job brings

Our family is living the American dream

My kids are in school

And I'm able to pay the bills

What else can I ask?

America has been our hope

Often I feel frustrated about a pay raise

But I still have a job

It's how I take care of my family

The best way I know

So on this day I'm most grateful!

"God, I have a thankful heart for a good job. And with my family I celebrate the joys of Labor Day that mean so much to us."

Amen

A Simple Life

People don't have to be religious to live simple lives.

Simplicity comes with commonsense

And by living according to life's affirming values

The good life is inspired by love

And it takes knowledge to make our goals realities

Spiritual texts speak about people's future

So that's why many of the religious choose this lifestyle

But for ordinary folks living simply calls for wisdom

They view earthly excesses as a burden that damages their welfare

So they pledge to themselves to live within their means

Simple people are enthusiastic about learning from nature

They do what's right to live in harmony with the natural forces

Some go to bed early in the evening after winding down

Others rise early in the morning when it's quiet for prayer

The sun, moon, and stars are planets that are celebrated.

The wind, birds, trees, lakes, and mountains teach life's affirmations

As well as the four seasons of spring, summer, fall, and winter

Nature's beauty grounds them physically, spiritually, and psychologically

Simple folk may strike some as though they are poor.

But by their way of living they are attuned to the rhythms of nature

They eat the best that nature offers, and live wisely by taking care of themselves

And many of these folks work tirelessly in the vineyards to bring peace to a broken world

"Great Emancipator, shine your light on those that live simple lives. Help them to blossom in their lifestyle so that others will see them as role models."

Amen

Faces of God

God is a paradoxical figure

This Being isn't a person

But the Creator of the world

God isn't only anthropomorphized

But a multiple of personalities

God is a Creator, Destroyer, Advocate

Deceiver, Trickster, Father

Woman, Protector, and Friend

In these combinations God often acts

Indecisively, erratically, and moodily

God destroyed his creations

In a flood that consumed the entire world

This Creator-God saved Noah and animals

Before showing a rainbow in the sky

Promising not to flood the earth again

Later God showed up as a warrior

Leading the Israelites out of Egypt

Across the Red Sea from Pharaoh

But God was vindictive

When He caused the Israelites

To wander for years in the desert

Bringing death and destruction

To those who disobeyed Him

"God of Abraham, Isaac, and Jacob you present believers with a polytheistic worldview of who you are. Yet the faiths of Judaism, Christianity, and Islam attest to being monotheistic. Why did you tell mankind to be fruitful and multiply but you went back on your own promises? Help us to understand your nature."

Amen

Recycling Creates Jobs

Recycling creates jobs

Its economic returns are well-documented

More than 757,000 people work in recycling

And they earn more that 36-billion dollars annually

There are many benefits in processing such materials Including
alumina, plastic, and soft drink containers

Steel cans, detergent bottles, newspapers, and trash bags

So consumers help when they purchase such items

These materials can be collected, processed

And manufactured into a variety of new products

But consumers should buy the right kind of recyclables

And they could have these materials collected

At curbsides, drop-off centers, or use refund centers

Remember recycling reduces the amount of waste to landfills

It helps conserve natural and valuable resources, and saves energy

Above all it creates jobs from which many workers benefit

Recyclables' costs go up and come down depending on supply

And recovery facilities sort these products for manufacturing

*"Loving Creator, help us to recycle our products. And guide consumers as good
stewards in caring for the environment, and providing jobs for many people."*

Amen

Small Gyms' Problems

The pandemic has upended small gyms

Many of these 40 000 to 50 000 health

And fitness clubs are in the U.S.A.

The International Health Racquet & Sportsclub Association

Estimates as of August 31, 2020 these gyms lost

Some 413.9 billion during the shut down

IHRSA warns that without government help

As many of as a quarter of these gyms could close

These small health and fitness clubs

Play an essential role in their clients' lives

People work out and keep fit to face daily challenges

Many of these gyms generally open at 5 a.m.

They serve their clientele until late at night

But the coronavirus pandemic is keeping many away

And some of these fitness centers decided to have online classes

But health facilities such as the small gyms

Follow the guidelines of the Centers for Disease Control and
  Prevention

These clubs space their bikes, and treadmills for social distancing

The equipment is disinfected after clients use them

And all participants are encouraged to wear masks

But these smaller gyms are really hurting

For their clientele base isn't large

So although these gyms employ some 3-million workers

Many of the trainers and instructors will have to be let go

"Divine Creator, help small gyms as they struggle with the effects of the coronavirus pandemic. And be with the clients that continue to use these facilities that they may do so safely."

Amen

Holiday Shopping

The coronavirus pandemic

Is surely making its mark

It's changing the way

People will shop during the holidays

Thanksgiving, Black Friday, and Christmas

Won't be the same for many this year

Stores such as Best Buy, Macy's, and Target

Are planning ways to safeguard the health of their consumers

So these businesses have decided to have early shopping

This shopping season will start in early October

And is meant for shoppers not to flock to the stores

Just cutting down on the dangers of them being infected

But uncertainties exist – will buyers' demand be as great?

The Covid-19 pandemic has brought quite a backlash

Many workers have been laid off, others furloughed

And while many more are working from home

Quite a few have lost their jobs with the downturn of the economy

Companies will use a variety of tactics to get consumers to buy their
    products

People could be expected to be steered to their stores' websites for deals

So consumers will have the option of shopping online

But businesses don't know what to expect because of the downturn

Some executives predict since people are spending less on travel and restaurants

There will be a great chance for online businesses such as amazon.com to pick up the slack

"Heavenly Provider, help businesses at this time of uncertainty as they cater for the needs of consumers during the holiday season. May shoppers act wisely and be safe as the crisis of the coronavirus pandemic rages."

Amen

Pandemic Blues

The coronavirus pandemic

Has struck with some drawbacks

It isn't always a rosy picture

As some people working from home find

Working parents are experiencing other trials.

They not only have the responsibility of their jobs

But they are bothered by the additional stress of childcare

Some of these adults are also in a bind of caring for aging parents.

As seniors they are quite vulnerable to Covid-19 infections

Quarantined parents have to schedule appointments for their loved ones

It's stressful thinking about risks, wearing masks, and social distancing

When attempting to shop for the necessities of life, and have doctors' visits

Its true there has been times when there are online medical visits

But working parents may have to leave the home to fill prescription medications

Other problems may arise if some employees are living alone

Some may feel exhausted by the isolation without communicating with friends

These individuals have no roommates with whom to share their problems

So they become distracted and overwhelmed by the demands of the pandemic

Changes to solo lives caused by the coronavirus add unexpected stress

Being bombarded by the social unrest on TV might well trigger anxieties

These swings of emotions could be caused by bad news which floods the airwaves

There have been natural disasters such as hurricanes and wildfires in regions of the country

"Infinite Reality, help us so that we don't become overwhelmed with the crises in our daily lives. Guide us to do our best to wisely face all uncertainties which arise when we are quarantined."

Amen

Human Trafficking

Human trafficking is an international problem.

Traffickers use many deceptive tricks

In order to hold humans against their will

Traffickers know these humans are poor

They come from mainly from the continents

Of Africa, Asia, and Latin America

These captives are generally young people –

Usually male and female

With women there are special problems

Many become pregnant in captivity

And often have to raise their children

Under quite deplorable conditions

As they labor to do the chores of their household

Slavery of this sort may last for a number of years

The humans in bondage are threatened with deportation

If they try to counter the harshness of their living conditions

But some have the opportunity to buck this trend

For they develop the courage to run away

Other might be rescued by active workers

From the American Anti-Slavery Group

"Universal Creator, who knows the hearts of all men and women, help those that are held in bondage to be rescued. And guide these poor people so that they will be able to adjust to the freedom of living a normal lifestyle."

Amen

Offices Won't Die

The coronavirus has struck

Offices have been impacted

And many are working from home

Will the office die?

That's a big question

Working at home has proved

To be attractive and comfortable as the workplace

Businesses are weighing these benefits

Considering if they should continue to invest in real estate

But the option of working from home is fluid

It's freeing for employees to be happier in this environment

Office work goes back to the days of the Industrial Revolution

Are employers going to move away from paper-pushing offices?

The pandemic has raised the question, "What form should the office take?"

With the rise of remote working many employees have latched on to the idea

But is this the end of the office as workers know it?

Office work has therefore become a hot topic of discussion

Will there be a paradigm shift in how the office used to be?

The pandemic has brought new insights about how employers should think

And it appears that working at home will make for a flexible model for the future

"Omniscient Creator, the pandemic has surely made its impact on workers around the world. Help the companies and employees determine what's best for all those concerned as they navigate this new reality."

Amen

O' Christmas Tree!

Oh what will I do without a Christmas tree?

Christmas tree growers are having problems

The harvest is lacking this year

And buyers are being turned away

It takes about twelve years for trees to mature

To be sold to the public

But these tree farms were depressed in 2008

There were forest fires on the West Coast

That has wiped out prospects of a good harvest

Other problems have arisen that impacted these growers

There has been drought due to climate change

On the East Coast infestation of these trees was a problem

So from East to West there are shortages

How can consumers get live trees this Christmas?

They have to deal with scarcity and higher prices

The trees therefore will be smaller

But they can still bring joy this Christmas

So shop early. Go to the tree farms

And be sure to be the first in line to select your tree

"Almighty Creator, you have provided Christmas trees to grace our homes. Help us as we face this shortage, and don't remove from our hearts the love of Christmas."

Amen

PART VI - PEACE PEOPLE EXPLORE

Religious Life

Many people who are religious have a faith tradition

The majority subscribe to one of the major faiths

But Judaism is the oldest monotheistic religion

This faith isn't considered major with many adherents

But it's most important because Christianity and Islam spun off of Judaic beliefs

The most popular religion that's worldwide in scope is Christianity

It's based on the Trinity – Father, Son, and Holy Spirit

Catholics venerate Mary, the Mother of God

This faith tradition is headed by a pope, and is known for its rituals, and saints

Islam follows Christianity in popularity

In this faith Muhammad the founder is a prophet

It's known for its orthodoxy, Five Pillars of faith, and pilgrimage to Mecca

But Hinduism has no known founder

It's polytheistic in nature with a pantheon of gods with diverse beliefs

And Buddhism though has no belief in a God

For a Buddhist attaining Enlightenment is a goal

In China there exists Confucianism and Daoism

These faiths teach living with authority, and practice filial worship

Daoism pursues "the way" as the true path

This pursuit is likened to the consistency of water that flows to undetermined places

While Japanese Shintoism with indigenous practices worship "kami"- people, places, and things

Secular Humanism arose on the European horizon during the Age of Enlightenment

It ushered in scientific perspectives in the understanding of God and nature

The works of Charles Darwin among others were to have a profound impact on its followers

The first parliament of religion was at the World's Columbian Exposition in Chicago in 1893

"Universal Spirit, let us honor the Golden Rule - the tenets of all religious beliefs in the world. 'Let us treat others the way we wish to be treated.'"

Amen

Seek Peace

Seek peace and illuminate your path

Cultivate a clean mind and contrite heart

Be blessed with the gifts of God

And be inspired to become a true light

Undertake a divine mission

Whether serving Allah, Brahma, or Dao

Walk down the right path

Keep moving and you'll make progress

Having faith leads to an enlightened heart

But remember the joys of this world are fleeting

Finding true peace is an enduring weapon

That paves the way of a successful life

With believers their future is bright

By living according to divine promises

And they become wise men and women

So hardships will be like pin pricks

Compared to the happiness awaiting the devout

The world is buffeted by change

Deviancy is found in sensual excesses

And worldly types live in the shackles of fickleness

So stay your course on the right path

In a world that's constantly trying to change you

"Divine Creator, help us to persevere in doing good in our communities. Guide our commitments to bring peace to the world."

Amen

Essentials of Peace

Live in peace and be secured

Refrain from strife

And don't be quick to quarrel

So depart from evil and do good

Let us be instruments of peace

Let our hearts sow love

By always offering the gift of compassion

These are the gestures of peacemakers

Peace is a journey that calls for many steps

So be sure to take a step at a time

But first people have to make peace with themselves

This is a question about living up to challenges

Let the power of love drown out the love of power

For its power that's the stumbling block in our lives

Only by recognition of this warped reality

Will artificial divisions between nations crumble

Peace can't be kept by force

It could only be achieved through understanding

So let nations come together at the bargaining table

Where their grievances could be ironed out

A negotiator's attitude is essential for successful talks.

"Almighty Advocate, help conflicting parties reach just agreements. Guide our nations so that they will discover true peace through patience, understanding, and dialogue."

Amen

Visitors in National Parks

Park visitors are stricken

By the pandemic that's causing havoc

In fall the temperature is cooler

And there's the annual ritual

Of trees displaying their colors

Leaves change to different shades

Of red, brown, yellow, and purple

This is the time to visit the national parks

Be it Acadia, Shenandoah

And the Great Smoky Mountains

But remember to wear your mask

Be prepared to practice social distancing

You can never tell who you'll meet on a trail

Be sure to plan your visits to avoid crowds

There's usually congested traffic

On stretches of the roadway

Of the Great Smoky Mountains Park

But the park campsites sites are adequately spaced

And the facilities are cleaned regularly

By using lesser known trails

Visitors will have the peace of mind

Of enjoying an environment of beautiful trees

And the many trails wherever they go

It'll be pretty and relaxing this time of the year

Although there'll be fewer park attendants

Taking care of critical resources

That park goers have come to enjoy

"Great Provider, be with park attendants during this pandemic. Help visitors so they will be able to enjoy the peace in the parks amidst the beautiful leaves of trees."

Amen

Lasting Peace

Let prayer be the light of your life

It's the only way to live under God's protection

It's wise to pray for divine guidance

Live triumphantly and shout for joy

Let "Shalom! Peace!" Be your battle cry

Accept that you might not always succeed

You may do your best and still not win

But with prayer just persevere

Set high goals to do what's right

It's your pleas on high for help that counts

Sooner or later your prayers will be answered

Prayer warriors should visualize the results

You should work at illuminating your goals

And always direct your beliefs to Allah, Brahma, or Dao

Have the peace that takes courage to bear fruits

And you'll receive an olive branch of tranquility

The most certain way to succeed is to pray without ceasing

Peace is what believers should always pursue

This is the basic truth about life's journey

Believers will be blessed with justice and secured hearts

And transient peace will pass them by

Love and compassion will triumph in the end.

*"Great Spirit, open our hearts to lasting peace. Help us as we journey
down the long and winding road that leads to personal fulfillment."*

Amen

Peace of Mind

What do people want?

Its happiness, health, and security

They long to have a good family

And their dreams fulfilled

So dedicate yourself to doing well

Desire these precious gifts

Age gracefully, and be at peace

Never mind if you lose your youth

It's what you have gained that is important

At an older age you've become wiser

You know that appearance isn't everything

As you've stepped into life's arena

The main destroyer of a peaceful mind is anger

So protect yourself when bombarded

With messages that pull down rather than build up

To fully enjoy life, explore your own breathing space

Then embrace success after doing your best

By becoming what you're capable of being

For it takes self-will to accomplish these goals

"Almighty Creator that dwells in the shelter of the Most High, guard our minds, and help us to experience peace that surpasses all understanding."

Amen

A Peacemaker's Role

Peacemaking is more than winning wars
A peacemaker isn't a nation's warrior
He or she should be beyond wars
This individual should love their country
And have its interests at heart

Peace often calls for patience
It's an ability to negotiate problems
A peacemaker has to be able to compromise
This should be the goal of every ambassador

Building bridges to other peoples and nations
Should be silver lining that a negotiator should pursue
It's how a ruler endeavors to leave such a legacy
But few of them will succeed if this isn't done wisely

Some ambassadors will do anything to pursue peace
Christian leaders will remember the admonition –
"Blessed are the peacemakers"
They will see peacemakers as children of God

These rulers will be judges among many people

And arbitrate between warring nations abroad

They shall beat their swords into plowshares

And used their spears as pruning hooks

They shall learn war no more

And their neighbors will be wise to compromise

"Omnipotent Arbitrator, help warring nations to seek peace and understanding. Guide their rulers as they negotiate so that they will secure a lasting peace."

Amen

Peace with COVID-19

How can the elderly be at peace with COVID-19?

It's killing them and reaping havoc in their midst

Yet people have to learn to live with the coronavirus

They should try to do so and find peace

With millions worldwide being affected by this virus

There are scams perpetuated during this pandemic

These are major incidents that cause many to stress

Especially the elderly that are sitting targets

But seniors must learn to protect themselves

So they don't lose it and sink into depression

Seniors should therefore have their families

And trusted friends looking out for their welfare

Don't let scammers try to talk them into their schemes

Telling them they have won a prize in a competition

And wanting them to pay taxes up front

But the elderly should remain calm and rely on loved ones

They shouldn't isolate themselves by living alone

But reach out to family and friends who are helpful

Dependence on trusted relatives brings comfort

They have to be at peace in this crisis

They can depend on the North American Securities Administrators Association

By reporting schemes that attempt to disrupt their life

To be widows and widowers shouldn't be seen as vulnerability

Know that scammers want to bleed them dry and drain their accounts

So they should be calm and be at peace when on social media

Don't answer telephone calls that ask for their personal data

All these incidents are red flags that they should report to the authorities

"Ever-loving Benefactor, help the elderly to be at peace when they are faced with schemes by scammers. Give them insight and guide them to detect these swindlers that seek to rob them."

Amen

Peace Blossoms

Let's greet the dawning
Of a new day
Let peace blossom
Like a rose in summertime

Know that the dew
Dropping on its petals
Are like crystals in our hearts
Glittering in the bright sunshine

This new reality
Tells us about love and peace
That enhances our being
And blesses us with hope

But peace is sacrosanct
Abiding in our world
It's the symbol of a white dove
Rising and darting amidst the stars
So let this new reality transform our hearts

"Heavenly Creator, lead us to know your lasting peace. Help people to strive to be champions of goodness in a broken world. And give us hope as we seek God's blessings in this world by what we are doing to promote a lasting peace."

Amen

Explore Peace

Don't let peace die
Breathe life into it
It's too precious to perish
Let the earth rejoice in peace

Peace has to be explored
In the streets and alleys of life
It's vital to keep it alive
Mankind's future depends on it
Without peace we'll fade away

So sound the trumpets from roof tops
Let these echoes resonate in villages
Peace is alive and well
As it marches in a parade for life
Let peace reign!

A noble peace all good people seek
It has to be based on compromise
With a golden heart everyone wins
This is the goal of embracing the truth
Let peace reign!

*"Almighty Negotiator, show us the way to resolve our problems. Guide
our hearts and minds to embrace what is true and just in life."*

Amen

PART VII - HOPE PEOPLE EMBRACE

Inspiration of Hope

Without hope there isn't fullness

Hope makes the world more habitable

People are blessed with caring minds

They respond to life's ups and downs with faith

But inspired hope calls for perseverance

People have to be steadfast in their goals

For their commitments to have the best results

They must practice love as an excellent virtue

Hope is like a flame that never goes out

Be inspired by this gift

And reach out to the world around you

Practice your faith with patience

Become a symbol of grace in your community

Seek this gift for its rewarding

Pray daily and storm the gates of heaven

Embrace knowledge to find this truth

And you'll be blessed with good character

This is the way to have a moral life

Be concerned with those living in the world

And use your godly weapon of trust

Issues affecting the weak have spiritual implications

So strive to promote the welfare of all

Such actions call for courage against evil forces

"Almighty Provider, help us to endure patiently against the onslaught of this world. Guide us as we proclaim the truth about the peace one finds in knowing God."

Amen

Optimist at Heart

Infuse your life with joy

Don't wait for good things to happen

Just turn on your happiness lever

And make your dreams come true

Whatever you do believe

Be sure to honor the Creator

Just don't be passive about your goals

But do what you can to have grace

Be sure to stay positive and happy

Plug away with all your might

And don't give up when the going is rough

There's always a silver lining

Behind every dark cloud waiting to reveal itself

So surround yourself with inspiring people

Let your imagination run wild about life

Soon you will discover some basic truths

That hope always triumphs in the end

Go wherever your story takes you

However dark and difficult is the theme

There will always be fulfillment and redemption

So you should be an optimist at heart

"Loving Redeemer, fill our hearts with hope as we traverse the rugged terrain of life. Guide our steps so that there will be positive outcomes."

Amen

Outdoor Classrooms

The 2020 pandemic has made its mark

Teachers are finding new ways to adjust

How could children learn during these trying times?

One way is to venture outdoors

Outdoor classrooms are springing up

For children on the European continent

Such attempts have come alive in many countries –

Denmark, Norway, Germany, and Slovenia

But what do such classes have in common?

These classes are located in forests

Children walk or cycle to these regions

They sit under trees to be taught

And teachers feel they are making real progress

Outdoor students are more relaxed about learning

They aren't fidgeting around

As is the case with an indoor classroom

And there are reports that they are learning better

Yet there exists some concerns

These classes are great for biodiversity

Children are able to examine insects in their environment

But the biggest problem has to be changes in weather

And having shelters when the storms of life arise

"Great Spirit, you are showing teachers diverse ways to instruct their students during this pandemic. Help them as they weigh the benefits and safety of indoor and outdoor instruction."

Amen

The Crucifix of Hope

The crucifix is important for Christians

It's the major symbol of their religion

It's a sign of hope

For it tells about the death, resurrection

And ascension of Jesus Christ

When believers adore the cross

They are expressing a basic truth of their faith

People might wear this emblem

To show that they are devoted to Christianity

Some may even wear a ring

With a gold cross engraved on it

Bookmarks with the crucifix

Are used by many readers of Christian texts

These are made of cardboard, and metal

They are often inscribed with a bible verse

And some believers and non-believers alike

Wear earrings adorned with a cross

In Christian churches crucifixes are at the altars

A large crucifix precedes the priest

As he or she enters or leaves the sanctuary

And Christians often will bless themselves

By making the sign of the cross

"Jesus Christ, you have blessed Christians with the crucifix as a symbol of their faith. Continue to grant them hope as they look forward to your heavenly salvation."

Amen

All Lives Matter

In positive ways

Influence the lives around you

Let us remember that all lives matter

Rather rich or poor, black or white

It's the life that counts

Some live affluent and carefree lives

Failing to notice those that are neglected

But these are the poor who deserve our attention

So make it your duty to care for them

Let your religion be very simple

Let it be one of kindness and compassion

Show goodness with pure and contrite hearts

And let these gifts be reflected in your spiritual lives

When people's thoughts are polluted

They descend in the depths of despair

So you should endeavor to love your neighbor

As though your whole life depends on it

And experience God's mercies and be faith-filled

Be a success and embrace those you meet

Make friends with everyone you encounter

And let such a motivation inspire you

To be a blessing to all men and women

Trapped by the complexities of modern-day culture

"Infinite Provider, help us to cherish all men and women. Let us do so without regard to class, color, religion, creed, or national origin."

Amen

Working from Home

Workers are experiencing an array of emotions

Brought on by the coronavirus pandemic

Their feelings are exacerbated in isolation

But many see hope by working at home

These home-bound workers

Are able to spend more time with their families

Their new schedule gives them more flexibility

They are enjoying the convenience of their own homes

Many have ventured out at lunchtime for walks

In working from home there's less distraction

Workers' productivity has greatly increased

McKinsey survey research finds that 41 percent

At their desk at home are more productive

Many introverts have benefited from changes in the work place

They are presently being able to judge by what they produce

And not by how they promote themselves at meetings

Working parents are happy to be spending time with their families.

They are able to be teachers of their kids who are taking remote classes.

Many have found new ways in practicing gratitude and being imaginative

Parents are more relaxed and are spending more time caring for their needs

"Great Emancipator, help all the families and friends that are quarantined by the coronavirus pandemic. Continue to guide them as they work from home in unison with their children as they face these trying times."

Amen

A Joyful Heart

Give thanks to the Almighty

For a joyful heart

A heart that embraces

The good things of our lives

These gifts can't be seen

But they surround us

Like the air we breathe

And how we feel every passing day

They are goodness, kindness, and truth

Attributes we feel with our hearts

So reach out to the splendor that surrounds you

Know that you aren't alone in this world

But you're surrounded by the grace of God

Build bridges that enlighten others

Light a lamp that shines in the entire world

And be at peace with everything you do

Put your heart, mind, and soul in the smallest acts

This is the way you'll find true joy

Small things do matter most in our lives.

"Universal Spirit, guide us in ways to live more fulfilling lives. Let our hearts be open to those things we don't see, but know that they will be in our best interest. Grant us peace, love, and joy.

Amen

Seeds of Hope

Just as how you plant
Sow seeds of hope in the land
It's always wise to prepare the soil
And to know what you're planting

It's best to sow good seeds
There isn't a need to be negative
Let the goodness in your heart sprout
To the delight of those you touch

Deeds don't necessarily have to be large
They can be small ones that matter
But let your appearance signal your intent
And put a loving smile on your face

Reach out and embrace those around you
Know that we're all interrelated
What interests you affects others
Having a pleasing disposition as a giver
Goes a long way with the gifts you wish to share
So continue to live in hope, share, and be blessed

*"Loving Savior, help us to live in hope even when the going is rough.
Open our hearts so that we can be conduits of grace to other people."*

Amen

Embrace Hope

What are you waiting for?

Don't you wish to be blessed?

What should you do?

Put your hope in God, Allah, Brahma, or Dao

Feel the warmth in knowing the Divine

Make your path straight in seeking the light

And embrace the celestial love that's all embracing

You're sons and daughters of the Most High

You've to love your neighbor as yourself

You've to walk steadfast in faith

And you'll be greeted by the Almighty One

It isn't any use being selfish in life

Share the joy you encounter with others

And foster goodness with those you encounter

So reach out to those that are lonely

It's the dawning of hope that counts

It entangles all difficulties that seek to entrap you

So let loose and rise like a star with brilliance

These gifts bear incredible blessings

"Divine Majesty, you've blessed us with many gifts. Let our hope and joys of the future surround us like the brilliance of the sun."

Amen

Black Lives Matter

An African American George Floyd died

In Minneapolis after being pinned to the ground

By an officer who pressed a knee into his neck

A national outrage erupted

Symbolic of the injustices Blacks experience

Demonstrations spread to cities throughout the land

Young and old protested police brutality

Protesters walked along the streets

Carrying signs venting their feelings

These demonstrators were lifting their voices

For all to see the pain that African Americans suffer

Their protests were for society to reckon

With the inequities of the American justice system

Protestors were calling for police reforms

They were opposed to the racial stereotyping

But they wanted law enforcement to be accountable

And Blacks not to be singled out

Because of the color of their skin

The social forces that opposed these protests

Argue that in America racial inequities don't exist

They say that there's equality of opportunity

While those that empathized with the demonstrators

Point to the legacy of slavery

And the injustices that continue to be perpetuated

"Omnipotent Benefactor, help Americans to come to grips with the legacy of slavery. Let all the good people of this land work for justice and equality for every man and woman regardless of their national origin."

Amen

Mother's Day Prayer

For Moms on Mother's Day

To all mothers, grandmothers, and great-grandmothers

You're special in our eyes

You're the ones who bore the children of nations

You're the women who undertake the brunt of the responsibility in our homes

In nurturing, loving, and shaping us to become the people we are

You've dedicated your lives to the tasks of raising us to be the best

And you pursue these goals with an all-encompassing love

The Universal Spirit has blessed you with the "Special Gifts of Motherhood"

You walked with your children in confidence raising us in the world

So the Eternal Spirit has graced you with teaching us what's right from wrong

And to be assets to the societies in both great and small nations

You've raised children in every land of different faiths –

Christians, Muslims, Buddhists, Hindus, and Taoists

Yet, although diverse, they live according to the Golden Rule

Yes, they are to "Do unto others as you would have them do unto you"

Great Spirit, you've gracefully blessed the mothers of our lands

And guided them to be the best parents

For such blessings husbands and children say

"Thank Divine Protector for your loving blessings of our outstanding mothers from the bottom of our hearts."

Amen

Father's Day Blessings

Holy Spirit guide our dads

That they may always do

What's right in your sight

Keep them safe

As they go about their daily lives

So that they may be at peace

Help them as parents of their children

And good husbands to their wives

Give them wisdom and understanding

To know what's best in these troubling times

Comfort them and walk with them

All the days of their lives

Universal Spirit, you who makes no distinction

Of race, color, or creed

Be with our dads in every home

Help them to be good mentors in their families

Teach them how to take criticism

When their efforts fall short

As dads, grandfathers and great-grandfathers

Bless and keep our dads

Universal Spirit, walk with them

Talk with them

And guide them

To be good leaders of their families,

Community and nation

"Eternal Presence by the grace of God, watch over our dads. Lift them up to be the best dads, grandfathers and great-grandfathers that they can be. For these blessings we pray."

Amen

Symbol of Change

Change is in the air

In America millions of voters took to the polls

They voted for their candidates

It's a decision to elect the president of the United States

And they cast their vote for a senator and congressman

But voters had many things on their mind

Some look at the character of their representatives

Some were concerned about the economy

Then there were those wishing for racial justice and harmony

Pollsters looked at the predominant white voters

Whether they were male or female

Their age group and identity were important

So most pollsters focused

On the choices of white men as opposed to white women

Rich or poor, and if they live in an urban or rural communities

Minorities were a special concern

For they constituted a significant portion of the electorate

Many Black and Hispanic voters have different cultural identities

Blacks are often concerned with multi-ethnic representation

While the Cubans in Florida view the effects of socialism as important

Since many of them have taken refuge in the United States from Cuban oppression

"Loving Creator, embrace the various desires for social change amongst the diverse ethnic groups of the United States. Guide its citizens to make good choices when they vote for their candidates on Election Day."

Amen

Theology Without Walls

Studying and knowing about God can be tricky

Society has built walls about such manifestations

People are aware of this in their churches, synagogues, and temples

But why not focus on spirituality free of barriers?

The concept of God is beyond description

God is everywhere and is involved with all aspects of our lives

So God can't be confined to the narrow definition of any one religion

God transcends reality and can't be divvied up

God is all in all, the Universal Creator who can't be tied down

God isn't patriarchal or matriarchal

God is inclusive of the male and feminine gender

So why don't religious institutions reflect this fact?

In some religions only males can be priests

And with some synagogues women can't be rabbis

The holy scriptures are written with a gender bias

There's still racial discrimination in many faith traditions

It's found in Christian churches where there's segregation

On Sundays, congregation reflects this racial divide

Buddhism is said to be classified by its racial orientation

Some American Buddhists see themselves differently from Asians
But why should there be such divisions in these faiths?

"God, help us not to build walls around our faith traditions. Let people see the light in honoring a faith without walls that institutions have constructed."

Amen

Coronavirus Vaccine

What a relief to this pandemic!

A vaccine from Pfizer

– BioNTech and Moderna

Americans will be inoculated

Against this virus that's raging

Healthcare workers and those in nursing homes

Will be first to receive these shots

It'll be an attempt to counter the rise

Of thousands of infections each day

And hundreds of thousands of those who have died

Once the entire population is inoculated

It's hoped that the American society

Will return to a new normal

Gone will be the days when people have to isolate

Wear masks, practice social distancing, and washing hands

The American society will rebound

People will return to their jobs

Especially those occupations where they work with the public

But expect some may continue working from home

Although offices that we know will still exist

Society will once again come alive

Gyms will be open for those to exercise

People will enjoy going to restaurants and dining in

There will be new realities concerning how people relate

No doubt Zoom will continue to be the norm

With all those communicating with families and friends

"Almighty Savior, we thank you for the development of the coronavirus vaccine. Undoubtedly we're grateful for all the lives that will be saved."

Amen

Happy New Year 2021!

Let the new tides roll in

2020 has been a disaster

With so many deaths and suffering

Many thousands have died in the world

And people were stricken with the coronavirus

But with the end of 2020

A new reality has begun to shine

Vaccines – Pfizer + BibNTech and Modena

Have come aboard to rescue us

Hooray! to the scientists who invented them

And kudos to the FDA for their approval

So 2021 is time to turn a new leaf

No longer will science be denigrated

There will be a move afoot

For the United States to join the Paris Climate Accord

Attention to climate change will be on the table

With the new president- elect Biden

This New Year promises hope for all

With the healing of political divisions

There will be a new focus in America

The marketplace will rebound again

With more jobs for the unemployed

Who have suffered through this pandemic

And many Americans once again will be able

To put food on their table and pay their rent

"God, help us in 2021. 2020 has been a tragedy of the worse kind. We have suffered with this pandemic, many thousands have died, and people suffered horrendously. Heal the inhabitants of this world and those of our beloved nation. And grant them peace and prosperity in the coming New Year."

Selected Bibliography

Adoff, Arnold. 1970. Malcolm X. New York, NY: Harper Throphy A Division of Harper Collins Publishers.

André, Christopher. 2011. Looking at Mindfulness: Twenty-Five Paintings to Change the Way You Live. New York, NY: Blue Rider Press.

Armstrong, Karen. 2014. Fields of Blood: Religion and the History of Violence. New York, NY: Alfred A. Knopf, Inc.

_____. 2010. Twelve Steps to a Compassionate Life. New York, NY: Random House, Inc.

_____. 1993. A History of God. New York, NY: Ballantine Books.

Atwill, Joseph. 2011. Caesar's Messiah: The Roman Conspiracy to Invent Jesus. Charleston, SC: CreateSpace.

Becchio, Bruno and Johannes P. Schadé, eds. 2006. Encyclopedia of World Religions. Concord, CA: Concord Publishing, AG.

Bettany, George T. 1890. The World's Religions: A Popular Account of Religions, Ancient and Modern. New York, NY: Ward, Lock & Co.

Bowker, John. 2015. World Religions. New York, NY: DK Publishing, Inc.

Brodd, Jeffrey. 2009. World Religions: A Voyage of Discovery (3rd ed.). Winona, MN: Saint Mary's Press.

Carson, Rachel. 1962. Silent Spring. New York, NY: Houghton Mifflin Company.

Coogan, Michael D., ed. 2012. World Religions. New York, NY: METRO BOOKS.

Crosby, Donald A. and Jerome A. Stone, eds. 2018. The Routledge Handbook of Religious Naturalism. New York, NY: Routledge Taylor & Francis Group.

Dawkins, Richard. 2008. The God Delusion. New York, NY: Houghton Mifflin Company.

Darwin, Charles. 1859. The Origin of Species. London: Odhams Press Limited.

Dowd, Michael. 2008. Thank God for Evolution. New York, NY: Viking Penguin Group.

Douglass, Frederick. 1845. Narrative of the Life of Frederick Douglass. Boston, MA: Anti-Slavery Office.

Du Bois, William E.B. 2015. The Souls of Black Folk. Irvine, CA: Xist Publishing.

Ellwood, Robert S. and Gregory D. Alles, eds. 2007. The Encyclopedia of World Religions (rev. ed.). New York, NY: Facts On File, Inc.

Feuchtwang, Stephan. 2016. Religions in the Modern World (3rd ed.). New York, NY: Routhledge.

Flinders, Tim. 2013. John Muir: Spiritual Writings. Maryknoll, NY: Orbis Books.

Fuller, Robert C. 2001. Spiritual but not Religious. Oxford, NY: Oxford University Press.

Hahn, Thich Nhat. 2004. The Thich Nhat Hahn Collection. New York, NY: Bantam Books and Parallax Press.

Halverson, Dean. 1996. The Compact Guide to World Religions. Ada, MI: Baker Publishing Group.

Harris, Sam. 2014. Waking Up. New York, NY: Simon & Schuster, Inc.

Hexham, Irving. 2011. Understanding World Religions: An Interdisciplinary Approach. Grand Rapids, MI: Zondervan.

Hitchens, Christopher. 2007, God is not Great: How Religion Poisons Everything. New York, NY: Hachette Book Group USA.

Hoskins, Janet A. 2015. The Divine Eye and the Diaspora: Vietnamese Syncretism Becomes Transpacific Caodaism. Honolulu: University of Hawaii Press.

Jefferson, Thomas. 1776. United States Declaration of Independence. Washington DC: National Archives and Records.

HH the Dalai Lama and Desmond Tutu with Douglas Abrams. 2016. The Book of Joy. New York, NY: Penguin Random House.

Mandela, Nelson R. 1994. Long Walk to Freedom. New York, NY: Little, Brown and Company.

Matthews, Warren. 2012. World Religions. Boston, MA: Cengage Learning.

McDermott, Gerald R. 2011. World Religions: An Indispensable Introduction. Nashville, TN: Thomas Nelson.

Miles, Jack. 1995. God a Biography. New York, NY: Random House, Inc.

Nadler, Steven. 2011. A Book Forged in Hell. Princeton, NJ: Princeton University Press.

Northrop, Filmer C.S. 1953. The Taming of the Nations. New York, NY: Macmillan.

Parrinder, Geoffrey, ed. 1985. World Religions: From Ancient History to the Present. New York, NY: Checkmark Books.

Partridge, Christopher. 2013. Introduction to World Religions (2nd ed.). Minneapolis, MN: Fortress Press.

Raymo, Chet. 2008. When God is Gone Everything is Holy. Notre Dame, IN: Sorin Books.

Robinson, Thomas A. and Hillary P. Rodrigues. 2014. World Religions: A Guide to the Essentials (2nd ed.). Ada, MI: Baker Academic.

Sacks, Johnaton. 2015. Not in God's Name: Confronting Religious Violence. New York, NY: Penguin Random House LLC.

Sharma, Arvind. 2006. A Guide to Hindu Spirituality. Bloomington, IN: World Wisdom, Inc.

_____. 1987. *Women in World Religions*. New York, NY: State University of New York Press.

Shouler, Kenneth. 2010. *The Everything World's Religion Book: Explore the Beliefs, Traditions, and Cultures of Ancient and Modern Religions* (2nd ed.). Avon, MA: Adams Media.

Sifton, Elisabeth. 2003. *The Serenity Prayer*. New York, NY: W. W. Norton & Company, Inc.

Smith, Huston. 1991. *The World's Religions, 50th Anniversary Edition*. New York, NY: HarperCollins Publishers.

Toropov, Brandon and Father Luke Buckles. 2011. *The Complete Idiot's Guide to World Religions* (4th ed.). New York, NY: Alpha Books.

Waley, Arthur. 1938. *Anelects of Confucius*. London: Allen & Unwin.

Washington, Booker T. 1907. *Up From Slavery*. New York, NY: Doubleday, Page & Co.

Wilkinson, Philip. 2017. *Visual Reference Guides Mythology*. New York, NY: Metro Books.

_____. 2016. *Visual Reference Guides Religions*. New York, NY: Metro Books.

Zaehner, Robert C., ed. 1997. *Encyclopedia of the World's Religions*. New York, NY: Barnes & Noble.

About the Author

Guyanese-born Erwin K. Thomas, Ph.D., was a professor and graduate director of Mass Communications & Journalism at Norfolk State University, VA. Thomas has published eleven books on the mass media, devotionals, and a novel. He and his wife Mary Barta reside in Virginia Beach, VA, where they are members of an ecumenical Church of Holy Apostles. Their son Matthew, and daughter-in-law Shannon live in Charlottesville, VA.

Website: https://www.amazon.com/author/erwinthomas

Email: dfurstane@gmail.com